THE FABULOUS LOST & FOUND

AND THE LITTLE SLOVAK MOUSE

WRITTEN BY MARK PALLIS
ILLUSTRATED BY PETER BAYNTON

NEU WESTEND
— PRESS —

For Kate Heartwin - MP

For Hannah and Skye - PB

THE FABULOUS LOST & FOUND AND THE LITTLE SLOVAK MOUSE
Copyright text © 2020 Mark Pallis and Copyright images © 2020 Peter Baynton

All rights reserved. This book or any portion thereof may not be reproduced or used in any manner whatsoever without the express written permission of the publisher except for the use of brief excerpts in a review.

First Printing, 2020
ISBN 978-1-913595-04-3
NeuWestendPress.com

THE FABULOUS LOST & FOUND

AND THE LITTLE SLOVAK MOUSE

WRITTEN BY MARK PALLIS
ILLUSTRATED BY PETER BAYNTON

NEU WESTEND
— PRESS —

In the middle of the big city is a tiny yellow building. If anyone loses anything, this is where it ends up.

It is called the Lost and Found.

Mr and Mrs Frog keep everything safe, hoping that someday every lost watch and bag and phone and toy and shoe and cheesegrater will find its owner again.

But the shop is very small. And there are so many lost things. It is all quite a squeeze, but still, it's fabulous.

One sunny day, a little mouse walked in.

"Welcome," said Mrs Frog. "What have you lost?"

"Stratila som čiapku," said the mouse.

Mr and Mrs Frog could not speak Slovak. They had no idea what the little mouse was saying.

What shall we do? they wondered.

Maybe she's lost an umbrella. Everyone loses an umbrella at least twice, thought Mr Frog.

"Have you lost this?" asked Mr Frog.

"Dáždnik? Nie," replied the mouse.

Then Mrs Frog remembered something that had been handed in a few months ago…

"Is this yours?" Mrs Frog asked, holding up a chunk of cheese.

"Syr? Nie. Smrdí!" said the mouse.

"Time to put that cheese in the bin dear," said Mr Frog.

"Maybe the word 'čiapka' means coat," said Mr Frog.

"Now where did I put that nice yellow one?"

"Got it!" said Mr Frog.

"Kabát? Nie. Stratila som čiapku," said the mouse.

She was starting to feel a bit frustrated.

"We need to keep trying," said Mrs Frog.

Nie šál.

Nie nohavice.

Nie pulóver.

Nie slnečné okuliare.

Nie topánky.

"Stratila som čiapku," said the mouse.

Nie tri knihy.

Nie štyri banány.

Nie päť kľúčov.

It was no good. A fat wet tear rolled down the mouse's cheek.

"How about a nice cup of tea?" asked Mrs Frog kindly.

"Milujem čaj." Vďaka," replied the mouse.
They sat together, sipping their tea and all feeling a bit sad.

Suddenly, the mouse realised she could try pointing.

"Čiapka!" she said.

"I've got it!" exclaimed Mrs Frog, leaping up.

"A wig of course!" said Mrs Frog.

"Nie parochňa," said the mouse.

Nie červená.

Nie blondínka.

Nie hnedá.

Nie viacfarebná.

Nie zelená.

"What about this?" asked Mr Frog, pulling back a curtain.

"Áno!" exclaimed the mouse.

Príliš malá.

Príliš veľká.

Príliš vysoká.

Príliš tesná.

"One hat left," said Mrs Frog, reaching all the way to the back of the cupboard.

"It couldn't be this old thing, could it?"

"Môja čiapka. Našla som čiapku! Ďakujem mnohokrát," said the mouse.

"Ah, so 'čiapka' means hat. Wonderful!"
Mr and Mrs Frog smiled.

And just like that, the mouse found her hat.

"Zbohom," she said, as she skipped away.
"Zbohom," replied Mr and Mrs Frog.

"I wonder who will come tomorrow?" said Mr Frog.
Mrs Frog put her arm around him.

"I don't know," she replied, giving him a squeeze,
"but whoever it is, we'll do our best to help."

LEARNING TO LOVE LANGUAGES

An additional language opens a child's mind, broadens their horizons and enriches their emotional life. Research has shown that the time between a child's birth and their sixth or seventh birthday is a "golden period" when they are most receptive to new languages. This is because they have an in-built ability to distinguish the sounds they hear and make sense of them. The Story-powered Language Learning Method taps into these natural abilities.

HOW THE STORY-POWERED LANGUAGE LEARNING METHOD WORKS

We create an emotionally engaging and funny story for children and adults to enjoy together, just like any other picture book. Studies show that social interaction, like enjoying a book together, is critical in language learning.

Through the story, we introduce a relatable character who speaks only in the new language. This helps build empathy and a positive attitude towards people who speak different languages. These are both important aspects in laying the foundations for lasting language acquisition in a child's life.

As the story progresses, the child naturally works with the characters to discover the meanings of a wide range of fun new words. Strategic use of humour ensures that this subconscious learning is rewarded with laughter; the child feels good and the first seeds of a lifelong love of languages are sown.

For more information and free downloads visit www.neuwestendpress.com

ALL THE BEAUTIFUL SLOVAK WORDS AND PHRASES FROM OUR STORY

stratila som čiapku	I've lost my hat	*červená*	red
dáždnik	umbrella	*blondínka*	blond
syr	cheese	*hnedá*	brown
smrdí	it stinks	*zelená*	green
kabát	coat	*viacfarebná*	multicoloured
šál	scarf	*čiapka*	hat
nohavice	trousers	*príliš vysoká*	too tall (f)
slnečné okuliare	sunglasses	*príliš veľká*	too big (f)
pulóver	sweater	*príliš malá*	too small (f)
topánky	shoes	*príliš tesná*	too tight (f)
jeden	one	*našla som klobúk*	I've found my hat
dva	two	*dakujem mnohokrát*	thank you very much
tri	three	*zbohom*	goodbye
štyri	four		
päť	five		
počítač	computer		
knihy	books		
kľúče	keys		
banány	bananas		
bicykle	bicycles		
milujem čaj	I love tea		
vďaka	thank you		
parochňa	wig		

THE WORLD OF
THE FABULOUS LOST & FOUND

THIS STORY IS ALSO AVAILABLE IN...

FRENCH   SPANISH
ITALIAN   CZECH
KOREAN   WELSH
GERMAN   HEBREW
SWEDISH   POLISH   CHINESE
VIETNAMESE   LATIN   PORTUGUESE

...AND MANY MORE LANGUAGES!

ENJOYED IT?
WRITE A REVIEW AND
LET US KNOW!

@MARK_PALLIS ON TWITTER
WWW.MARKPALLIS.COM

@PETERBAYNTON ON INSTAGRAM
WWW.PETERBAYNTON.COM

Printed in Great Britain
by Amazon